Feline Boulevard

To my ever-cool dad Conrad Hamanaka, my forever friend Kalluk (aka "Mr. K"), Sachiko's grandfather DoDo, and Ava's beloved Kamie. You all joined the ancestors much too soon.

Furball Lane

Shelter Avenue

Purring Lane

Written and Illustrated by:
Sheila Hamanaka

Animal Welfare Institute
900 Pennsylvania Avenue, SE
Washington, D.C. 20003
www.awionline.org

ISBN: 978-0-938414-87-2
LCCN: 2010934459
Printed in the United States

Design by:
Ava Rinehart and
Cameron Creinin

KAMIE CAT'S TERRIBLE NIGHT

Animal Welfare Institute

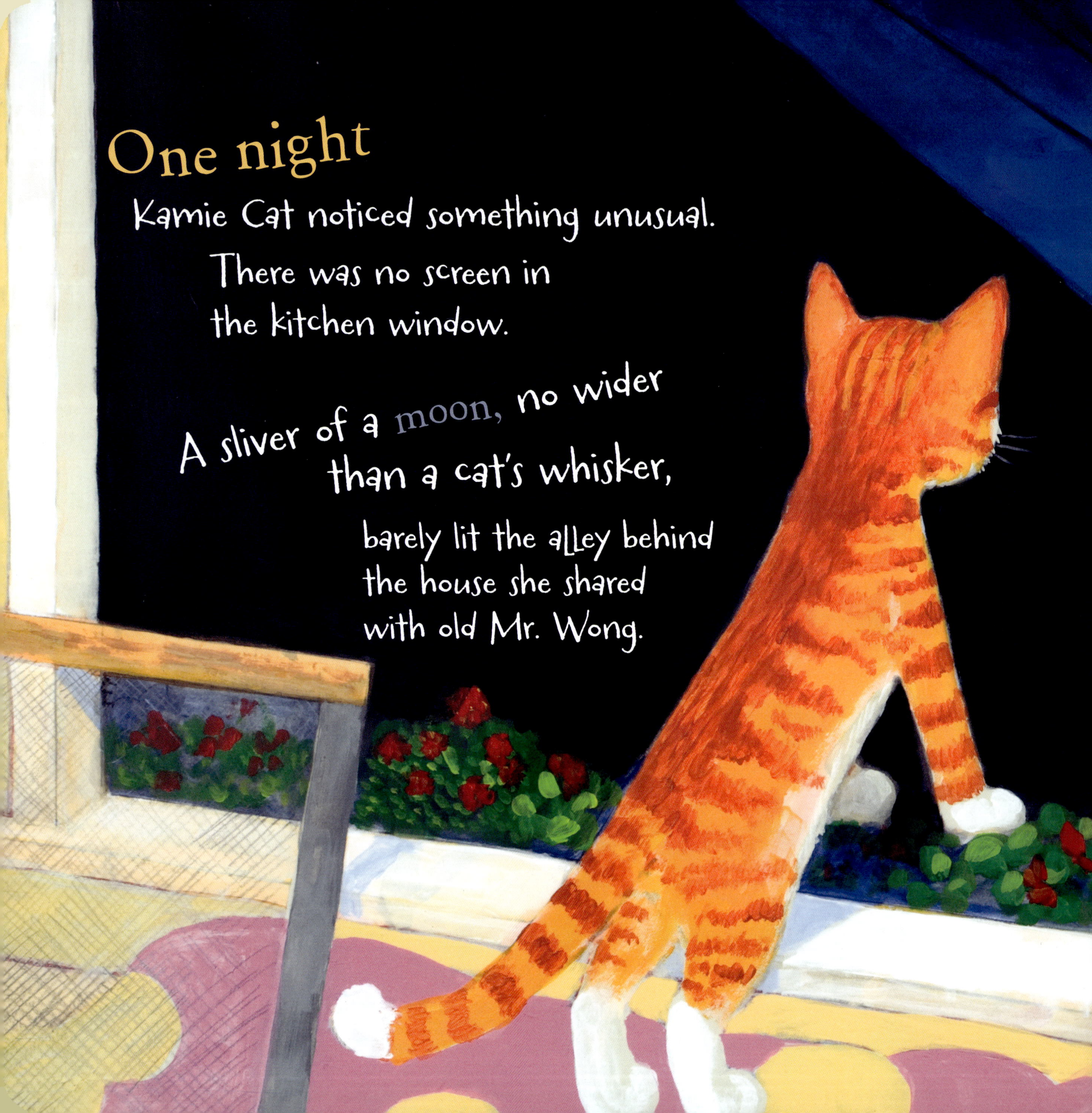

One night

Kamie Cat noticed something unusual. There was no screen in the kitchen window.

A sliver of a moon, no wider than a cat's whisker, barely lit the alley behind the house she shared with old Mr. Wong.

Music and the delicious smell of fried fish floated in on the night air.

Someone was having a party!

Kamie had never been to a party, and fish was her favorite food.

Quicker than a wink, Kamie Cat went out through the open window.

It was a big mistake.

From the other end of the alley, Kamie saw a big, black shape charging toward her. A dog!

He, or she, was barking like crazy.

She ran through one backyard, and then another.

She ran up a tree, but unfortunately it was a small tree.

The dog jumped up and knocked her to the ground. Kamie Cat landed on her feet and ran... right into the street!

Something even bigger and faster than the dog was headed right toward her!

It had two big eyes, each one brighter than the full moon!

Kamie ran and climbed over fences, garbage cans, and gazebos.

Fortunately, the dog and the thing with big yellow eyes were gone.

Unfortunately, Kamie was lost. And lonely.

How she missed her best friend, Mr. Wong!

In Kamie's neighborhood all the little houses looked the same.

Was this her house? Kamie peeked inside.

Yum!

A woman was serving her cat fresh food and water in clean bowls.

"MEOW!" Kamie yowled. "I'm hungry, too!"

The woman looked up. But instead of inviting Kamie to dinner, she yelled,

On the next block
she peeked
into another
window.

Inside,
a little boy was brushing
a cat with a
soft brush.

Kamie sighed.

Mr. Wong brushed
her every day!

Kamie almost meowed
but she remembered
how the lady had
yelled at her.

She kept going.

At the next house
Kamie watched a man
clean a cat box.

He filled it with fresh litter.

"There you are, Princess," the man said to his cat friend.

"I know cats are clean and like a nice, clean litter box."

Mr. Wong cleaned Kamie's litter box every day.

He loved Kamie,
and Kamie loved him.

It was very late now.
At the next house Kamie saw two cats curling up in a nice, round cat bed.
Mr. Wong had made Kamie a bed from an old basket. How she missed her soft, warm bed!

Sadly, Kamie moved on to the next house.

But it wasn't their house.

Inside, a cat was scratching the arm of a sofa.

A man who was sitting across the room began to yell. Then he threw a slipper at the cat!

Kamie frowned.

Mr. Wong always made sure that Kamie had a scratching post. He knew that cats need to scratch.

And he never, ever yelled at Kamie.

He never hit Kamie, either, or threw anything at her, even if she made a mistake.

Mr. Wong was kind.

Kamie ran away from the house.

Kamie hid under some bushes.
She began to cry.

"Here, Kitty!" someone said in a soft voice.

A young woman bent over and picked Kamie up.

"I think you are lost!" she said.

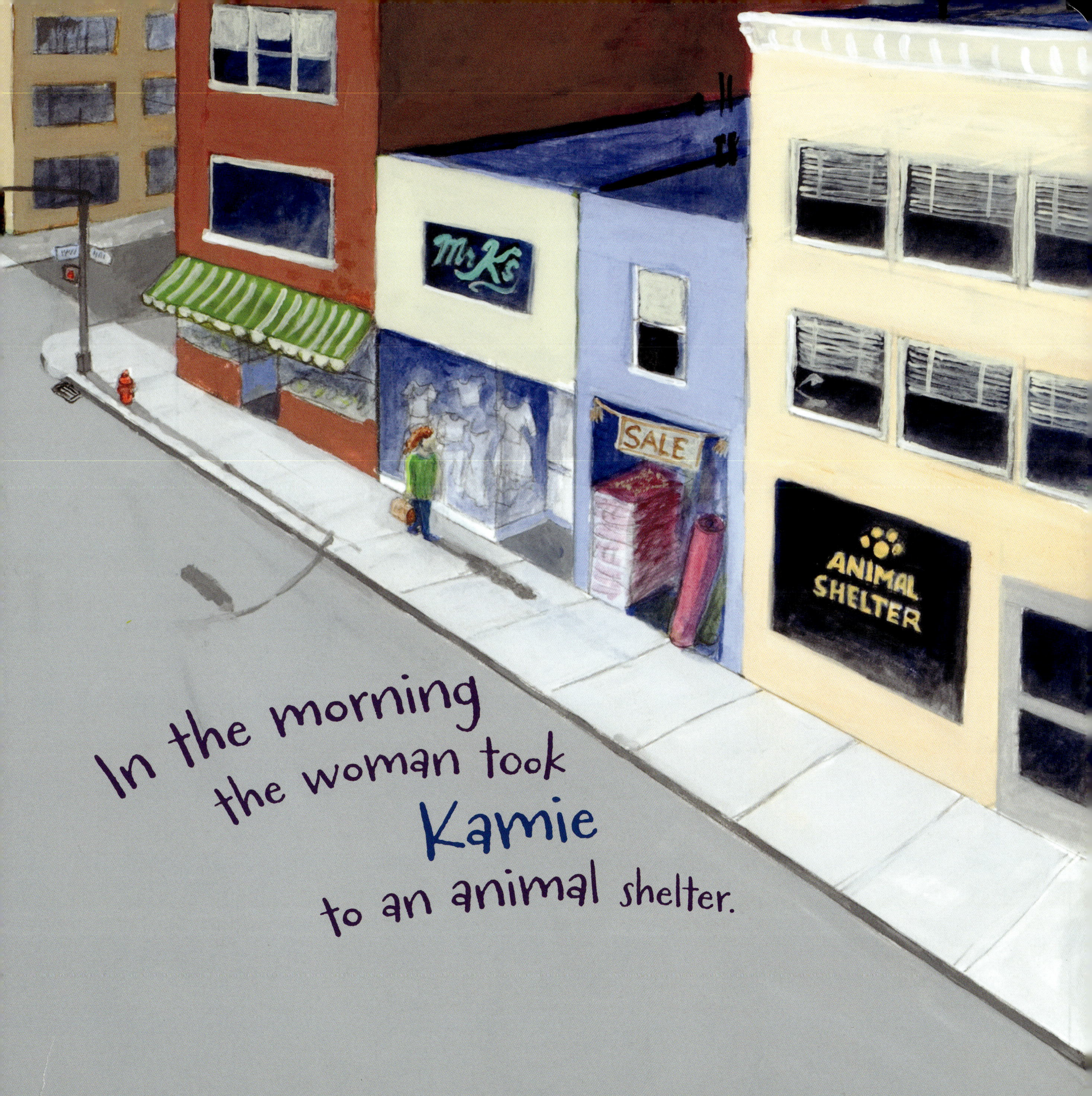

In the morning the woman took Kamie to an animal shelter.

"We're a bit crowded, but come on in," the veterinarian at the shelter said.

"No tag?" he said to Kamie.

"How are we supposed to know where you live?"

"I think she's old," said the young woman.

"Yes," said the veterinarian.

"And most people want to adopt cute little kittens," he added.

"Hmmm... she looks kind of scruffy, wouldn't you say?"

"No!
I would say she looks beautiful!"
a voice called out.
"And old is good.
An old friend is the
best friend of all!"
It was Mr. Wong!
He had come to the
shelter to look for her!
Kamie meowed
for joy.

"I'm sorry," said Mr. Wong.

"I'm sorry I forgot to put the screen in the window!

I'm sorry I didn't give you a collar with a tag on it so people would know where you live.

It will never happen again."

That night
Kamie and Mr. Wong
sat in the kitchen
after a fine dinner of fried fish.

The moon was no wider than two cat whiskers and the alley behind the little house was quiet and dark.

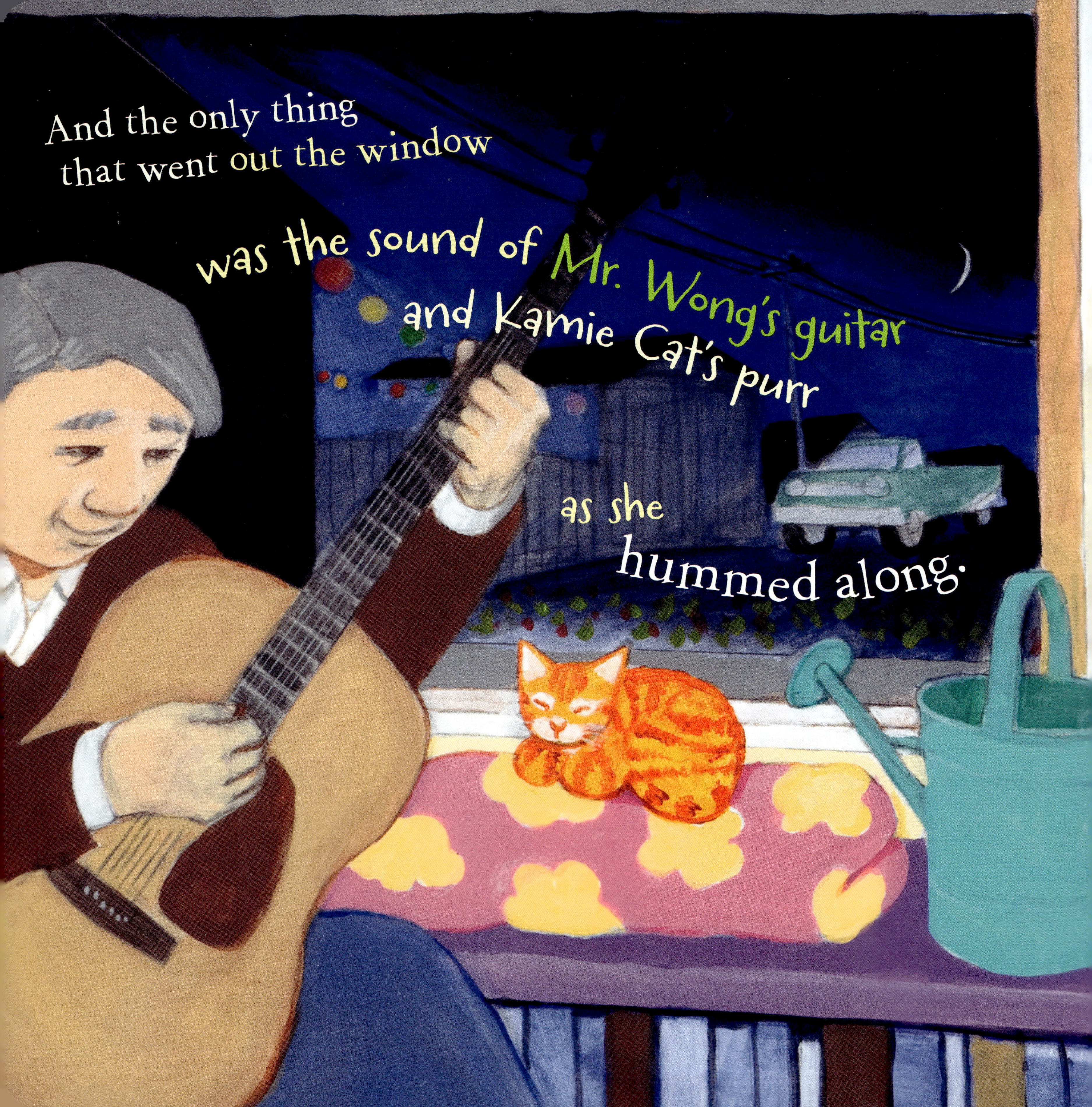

And the only thing that went out the window was the sound of Mr. Wong's guitar and Kamie Cat's purr as she hummed along.

About the Animal Welfare Institute

The Animal Welfare Institute (AWI) was founded in 1951 and is dedicated to alleviating suffering inflicted on animals by humans. AWI helps a wide range of animals in need, including those used in experimental laboratories, confined to factory farms, caught in steel traps in the woods, and threatened with extinction across the globe—from the smallest mice to the great whales of the sea. We believe that each person can make a difference for the animals by stepping up to help those who are suffering or are in need of a little assistance. Please consider becoming a member of AWI and helping us make the world a better place for all living creatures. For more information, including educational materials for children, visit AWI at: www.awionline.org.

 Mr. Wong's House

 Animal Shelter

Get Directions

About the Author–Illustrator

1. Sheila Hamanaka is an award-winning children's book author-illustrator whose work focuses on **multiculturalism** and **peace**. 200ft

2. Her books include the popular *All the Colors of the Earth; The Journey: Japanese Americans, Racism, and Renewal; Grandparents Song;* and *Bebop-A-Do-Walk.* 3mi

3. Deeply concerned about our **fellow animals** and the future of our planet, Hamanaka wrote and illustrated two other books for the Animal Welfare Institute: *The Boy Who Loved All Living Things: The Imaginary Childhood Journal of Albert Schweitzer* (2006), and ***Pablo Puppy's Search for the Perfect Person*** (2008). 500ft

4. She is currently working on a novel for middle grade readers. She lives in New York City. 5mi

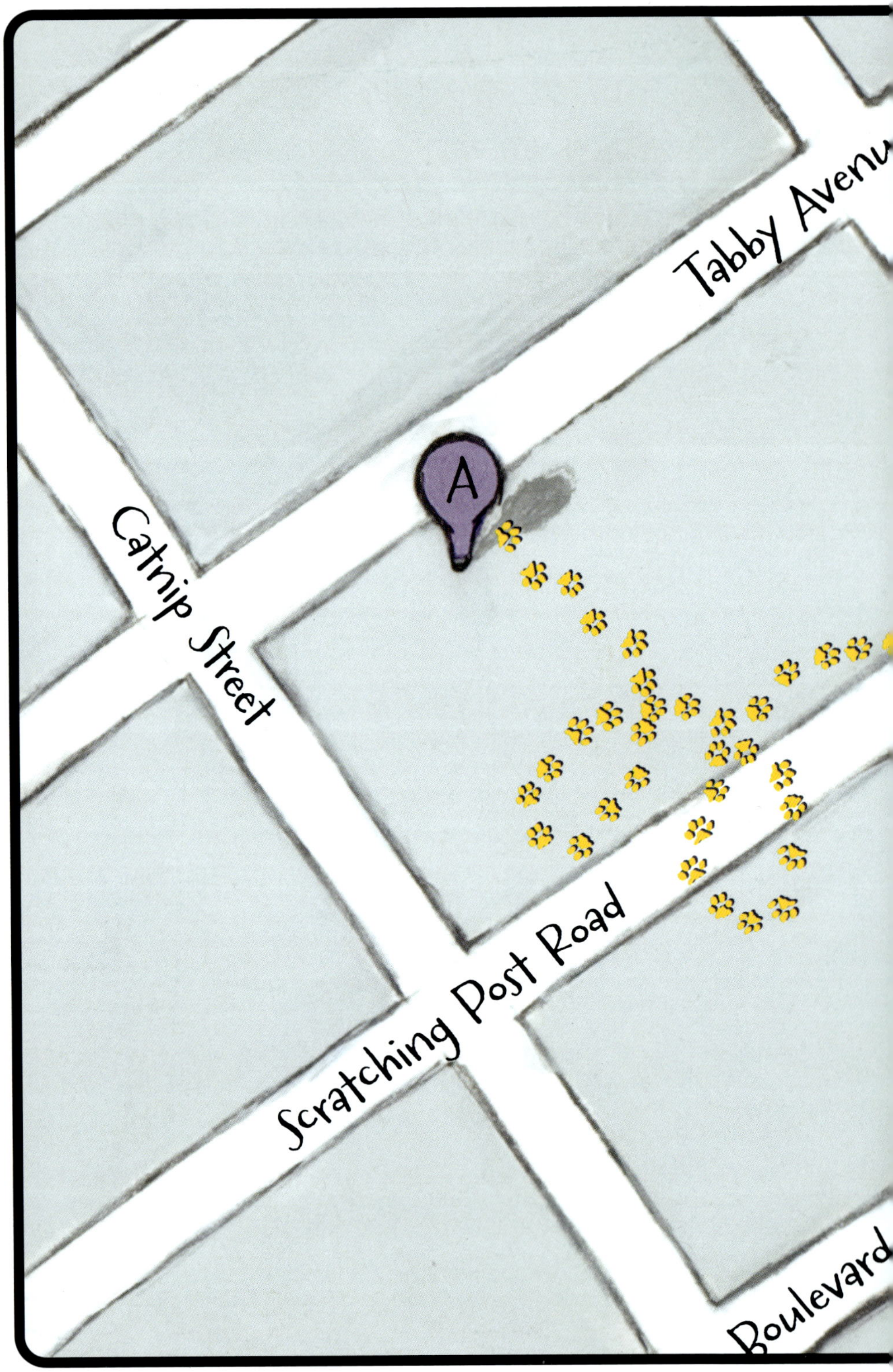

Tabby Avenu

A

Catnip Street

Scratching Post Road

Boulevard